Lawrence BROWN

The Somme

four years of fighting

List of contents

OREP
EDITIONS

Zone tertiaire de Nonant - 14400 BAYEUX
Tél. : 02 31 51 81 31 - Fax : 02 31 51 81 32
Email : info@orepeditions.com
Site : www.orepeditions.com

Editor: Grégory PIQUE
Graphic design: OREP
Layout: Laurent SAND
ISBN: 978-2-8151-0292-6
Copyright OREP 2017 - **Legal deposit:** 1st quarter 2017

INTRODUCTION

The Somme department in northern France has been the theatre of many conflicts. Modern warfare first arrived in 1870 during the Franco-Prussian war with fighting at Villers-Bretonneux and Pont-Noyelles. The losses suffered in these engagements were a taste of what was to come 44 years later.

The war of movement in August 1914 rapidly brought fighting to the Somme as the Germans executed their Schlieffen Plan that aimed to sweep around the French flank and take Paris, thus knocking them out of the war before concentrating on defeating the Russians.

Following the Battles of the Frontier, the French armies and the small British Expeditionary Force (BEF) began withdrawing. The Germans entered Péronne, a town on the river Somme on 28 August and a series of short but terrible engagements took place as the French fought bravely to stem the German tide. Amiens fell to the German *IV. Reserve-Korps* on 31 August but was liberated on 11 September by the French *81ème régiment d'infanterie* as the Germans pulled out following their

defeat on the Marne. Fighting returned to the Somme at the end of September as both sides attempted to outflank each other. As the fighting moved north, both sides began to dig in and the frontline would remain virtually unchanged until the Franco-British offensive of 1916.

The fighting would return to the Somme in 1918 as the Germans pushed back the British 5th Army across the former battlefields. The Somme would be the starting point of the final Hundred Days Offensive that pushed the German armies back to where it had all began in the hot summer of 1914.

This publication will look at various sectors and give a brief description of events that took place there throughout the four years of conflict.

German artillerymen bivouacking during the advance of 1914.

ALBERT

The industrial town of Albert sits astride the small river Ancre which winds its way from Miraumont in the north to the river Somme at Corbie. Following heavy fighting a few miles to the east the previous day, elements of the German *IV. Reserve-Korps* entered the town on 29 August 1914. The Germans eventually withdrew from Albert on 14 September 1914 following the victorious allied counter-attack on the Marne. With their Schlieffen Plan in tatters, the Germans now began to probe forward once again, this time from the Cambrai region with the Württemberg *26. and 28. Reserve-Divisionen* advancing astride the Albert-Bapaume road.

French troops were rushed into the area, many hailing from Brittany, and halted the German drive a few kilometres from the town. The fighting then moved north as the allied and German armies attempted to outflank each other. The lines would remain static in front of the town until the summer of 1916.

Albert remained in French hands until the arrival of British divisions in the sector in July 1915. It suffered severe damage from shell fire. The town remained within range of enemy guns until October 1916. Fighting

returned to the area in March 1918 following the German *Michael* offensive. The town, an important supply hub, was captured by the Germans on 26 March 1918 and remained in their hands until the ruins were liberated by the British 18th (Eastern) Division on 22 August.

The Basilica of Notre-Dame de Brebières was built in the late 19th century. A German shell toppled the golden figure of the Virgin Mary and baby Jesus in January 1915. Superstitious soldiers believed that if it fell this would herald the end of the war. It eventually fell due to British shell fire on 16 April 1918.

Albert had a population of 7,343 in 1914. In 1919 there were only 120 inhabitants.

What to see

Albert is an excellent starting point for any visit of the Somme battlefields. There are many art-deco buildings dating from the reconstruction period. The Somme 1916 museum evokes the fighting on the Somme in an atmospheric underground setting with numerous artefacts. The town hall bears a memorial plaque to the Machine Gun Corps, inaugurated a few months before the beginning of the Second World War...

Cemeteries – Albert French Cemetery with 6,294 graves. Albert Communal Cemetery Extension with 908 Commonwealth graves. One can see graves of men lost to tunnelling and mine activity at La Boisselle. Row D has a communal grave to 13 men of the 10th Essex killed by a German mine at the Glory Hole in November 1915.

OVILLERS-LA-BOISSELLE 1914-1915

The road from Albert to Bapaume leads you over a gentle rise that overlooks the valley in front of the villages of Ovillers and La Boisselle. It was here that the frontline settled at the end of September 1914 and both villages remained in German hands until July 1916.

The first units to fight in La Boisselle were the German *120. Reserve-Infanterie-Regiment* (Württemberg) and the *137ème régiment d'infanterie* from the Vendée region on 28-30 September, followed by elements of the French 22nd Division, notably the *64ème régiment d'infanterie* from Brittany. No further advance was achieved by either side and trenches were soon dug.

The French launched an attack against the two villages on either side of the main road on 17 December 1914. The Breton *19ème* and *118ème* R.I. were tasked with the attack, the objective of which was to capture Pozières and to draw attention away from planned offensives in the Artois and Champagne regions. The German defenders of *RIR 119* poured concentrated fire into the brave Bretons. The *19ème R.I.* lost 300 men killed and 800 wounded or taken prisoner for no gain.

"*My battalion, along with the two others of the 19th regiment were ordered to die and we went*". Commandant Viotte, C.O. of the 2nd Bn. 19ème R.I.

most fiercely contested areas of the Western Front in 1914-15. It later became known to the British as the Glory Hole. Mine warfare started here on 6 January with a German mine ; the French blew a charge followed by a failed three-company attack on the 10th. The Germans could hear further mining activity and blew a counter charge the next day which also set off the explosives in a French mine, sending up scores of French infantry into the air. The Germans of RIR 120 were appalled by the masses of half-buried French soldiers and organised a truce and even took wounded Frenchmen back to their own medical dug-outs.

Mine warfare continued with the arrival of the British in July 1915 when they took over the sector from the French.

The area of the ilôt and its mine craters can still be seen today.

« L'îlot »

The ilôt was the name given by the French to an area just in front of La Boisselle which became one of the

German Picklehaube   French 1884 képi

1916

The British took over the Ovillers – La Boisselle sector in August 1915. One of the first accounts of the trenches here was written by Lt. Charles Douie of the 1st Dorsets (32nd Division).
"*Liquid slime washed over and above our knees; tree trunks riven into strange shapes lay over and alongside the trench. The wintry day threw greyness over all. The shattered crosses of the cemetery lay at every angle about the torn graves, while one cross, still erect by some miracle, overlooked the craters and the ruins of La Boisselle. The trenches were alive with men, but no sign of life appeared over the surface of the ground. Even the grass was withered by the fumes of high explosive. Death indeed, was emperor here.*"

> **"My battalion, along with the two others of the 19th regiment were ordered to die and we went". - Commandant Viotte, C.O. of the 2nd Bn. 19ème R.I.**

The 174th Tunnelling Company (Royal Engineers) arrived in the Somme on 24th July 1915, setting up headquarters in Bray sur Somme before taking over former French mine shafts at Fricourt, Maricourt, Carnoy and La Boisselle.

Work began on the Lochnagar mine in November 1915 by the 185th TC, and was completed by the 179th TC. When the tunnel approached the German Schwaben Höhe salient, the tunnel was split into two forks and chambers at either end were filled with a total of 27,000 kg of ammonal explosives at a depth of 16 metres.

Lochnagar crater is one of the most visited sites on the Somme battlefields. It was purchased by Richard Dunning in 1978 and thus saved from the fate of the Y-Sap crater which has since been filled in.

1 July 1916

The Lochnagar and Y-Sap mines were blown at 7.28. Two minutes later, the infantry of the 34th Division left their trenches and began the slow advance towards the German lines. Despite the mines, the German defenders were able to set about the grim task of mowing down the slowly advancing British infantry. The 34th Division was a New Army division and many of its men came from the Newcastle area. Its losses were the heaviest of 1 July 1916 with 6,380 casualties. The 8th Division, attacking across 700 metres of No Man's Land, failed to capture Ovillers and suffered 5,121 casualties.

Ovillers finally fell to the 32nd ,25th and 48th Divisions on 15/16th July following a heroic stand by the German *15. RIR.* La Boisselle fell to the 19th Division on 4 July.

Men of the 34th Division advancing on 1 July 1916.

Splendid British Charge at La Boisselle

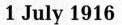

TRAGEDY OF D.S.O.

Lt.Col. Sandys of the 2nd Middlesex was wounded on 1 July in the 8th Division's attack on Ovillers. He committed suicide whilst convalescing in London two months later, unable to come to terms with the losses suffered by his battalion.

Lieutenant-Colonel E. T. Falkner Sandys, D.S.O., who committed suicide. He was wounded five times, and told a friend he wished he had died with his men during the offensive. He was in the attack on July 1.

What to see

The village of La Boisselle has memorials to the 34th and 19th Divisions, the Lochnagar crater can be accessed at any time. As you go past the Tyneside Scottish and Tyneside Irish Memorial you will be able to see the ilôt/Glory Hole sector to your right as you enter the village. This is private land and cannot be visited without permission. Ovillers has a Breton Memorial to the men of 19ème R.I. killed on 17 December 1914. Ovillers Military Cemetery has 3,436 British and 120 French graves. It started as a cemetery next to a dressing station before Ovillers was captured. The remaining graves are the result of post-war concentration.

POZIÈRES

Pozières main street in 1915.

The village of Pozières lies on a high ridge traversed by the Albert-Bapaume road.

The war briefly swept through the village as the Germans pushed on towards Amiens late August 1914. During the outflanking phase, following the Battle of the Marne, the German *XIV. Reserve-Korps* advanced down the main road as French troops, who had arrived a few days earlier at the Amiens railhead, prepared to halt their advance. On 27 September, German elements of *RIR 120* and *R119* were met with fierce resistance put

The village of Pozières in August 1916.

up by two companies of the *22ème régiment territoriale* but they pulled out the following day and the village would remain in German hands until the summer of 1916.

The battle for Pozières began on 13 July 1916 following the capture of the nearby villages of Ovillers and Contalmaison. These small attacks achieved nothing but high casualties. The next large-scale attack began on 22 July with the 1st Australian Division and the British 48th Division. The ruined village was captured and the Germans withdrew to their O.G. defence lines to the north and east of the village. The German high command ordered the recapture of Pozières and began to pour concentrated artillery fire into the rubble. It was said that the Australians experienced the heaviest artillery barrage of the entire war here. When the 1st Australian Div. was relieved on 27 July, it had suffered over 5,000 casualties. The nightmare was not over for the Australians ; the 2nd Australian Div. was next in the

"Pozières ridge is more densely sown with Australian sacrifice than any other place on earth." Charles Bean, Australian official historian.

What to see

Just before the village is the Pozières Military Cemetery with 2,756 graves and the Memorial to the missing of the 4th and 5th Armies of 1918 with 14,644 names. Upon entering the village there is a memorial to the King's Royal Rifle Corps, a little further along is the lane that became known as Dead Man's Road. The 1st Australian Div. Memorial is next to the former German Gibraltar strongpoint. Passing through the village, the Australian Memorial stands on the site of the windmill where the O.G. lines passed on Hill 160. Opposite is the Tank Corps Memorial, it was from here that two tanks first went into action on 15 September 1916.

"In the morning we had to advance to La Boisselle (from Pozières) over an absolutely flat stretch of ground and found bodies of French soldiers who had been hit by our shrapnels". Hans Ludwig 6/R120.

line and in two days lost 3,500 men. A fresh attack on the O.G. lines was made on 4 August and succeeded in their capture. The Australians now controlled the ridge and could see unspoilt countryside towards Courcelette and Bapaume. The 2nd Div. was relieved by the 4th Australian Div. on 5/6 August and in its twelve days in the line, had suffered 6,848 casualties. The Germans made one last attempt to recapture the vital high ground but were repulsed by the Australians in a fierce hand-to-hand fight. By the end of the battle, Pozières was nothing but a crater field strewn with the dead of both sides. The area was lost again in March 1918 and retaken by the 17th Division on 24 August.

Mouquet Farm

The road from Pozières to Thiepval takes the visitor past the site of what was perhaps the most fought over ground during the Somme battles. Mouquet Farm, known as Moo-Cow Farm to the Australians, sits on a ridge overlooking the valley in front of Thiepval. The farm today is sited to the right of the original emplacement.

The farm became a regimental headquarters to the various regiments of the German *26. Reserve-Division* and was used as a signalling station for German artillery during the failed British attack on Thiepval. As the fighting progressed and nearby Pozières fell to the Australians, Mouquet Farm protected vital high ground that prevented any progression, via the rear, towards the Thiepval strongpoint that had held off all attacks since 1 July.

The 16th Battalion of the 4th Australian Division was the first to go into action at Mouquet Farm on 10 August, they made gains but were subjected to an artillery barrage of unprecedented ferocity. The 2nd Australian Div. came into the line here on 22 August, followed by the 4th Australian Div. on 3 September who captured the farm, but discovered that the Germans had built an inter-linking defensive network below ground. A German counter-attack pushed them back again.

Australian soldiers.

The Australians were relieved in the Mouquet Farm – Pozières sector by the Canadian Corps on 5 September. Total Australian casualties were in excess of 23,000. The Canadians captured part of the farm on 16 September but were repulsed by a German counter-attack. The battered ridge and underground defences were finally captured by the British 11th Division on 26 September.

Australian leather infantry equipment.

"The flayed land, shell–hole bordering shell–hole, corpses of young men lying against the trench walls or in shell–holes; some – except for the dust settling on them – seeming to sleep; others torn in half; others rotting, swollen and discoloured." Charles Bean, Australian official historian.

Australian steel helmet with 14th Battalion, 4th Division insignia.

What to see

The present-day farm cannot be visited. Near the driveway is an Australian Imperial Force plaque commemorating the sacrifice of so many men around the Mouquet Farm sector.

COURCELETTE

The desolation of the Courcelette battlefield.

Courcelette lies in the valley beyond Hill 160 on the edge of Pozières. It was occupied on 27 September 1914 during the *26. Reserve-Division* during their drive towards the river Ancre.

Following the Australians' hard-fought victory at Pozières, the next phase of the Somme operations called for a large-scale offensive between Pozières and Longueval. The capture of Courcelette fell to two Canadian divisions. They had first arrived on the Somme sector on 5 September, taking over from the Australian Corps.

The attack was launched on 15 September 1916 and the 2nd and 3rd Canadian Divisions, supported by tanks which were being used for the first time in history, fought their way into the village and the strongly-held ruins of the sugar factory on the Albert-Bapaume road. The Canadians would remain in the area until the close of the Somme battles in late November. The Germans held on stubbornly to Zollern Graben trench near Mouquet Farm and Fabeck Graben near Courcelette. October-November saw some of the grimmest fighting along the high ground north-east of the village where the Germans held Regina Trench, a defensive line that used a new defensive doctrine of being below the skyline and thus out of direct artillery observation. The first attempt to take it was made on 1 October and it was not until 11 November that it was finally captured by the 4th Canadian Division. The final phase was an attack on Desire Trench on 18 November. Total Canadian casualties in the Courcelette area were in the region of 24,000.

The area was back in German hands in March 1918 and was recaptured by the 10th Lancashire Fusiliers on 24 August 1918.

"My platoon was in the third and last wave of the advance. We crawled over the parapet and lined up on a broad, white tape....it was almost Zero Hour. I looked at my wrist watch and saw we had about three minutes to go. I never heard our officers' whistles to signal the advance, and I don't suppose they heard them either because of the terrific crash with which the creeping barrage opened up, exactly at 6.20 am." Private Lance Cattermole, 21st Battalion, 2nd Canadian Division. Courcelette, 15 September 1916.

1st Canadian Division signaller's tunic and helmet.

Canadian pocket knife found near the site of Regina Trench.

What to see

The Canadian Memorial of Courcelette stands on the main Albert-Bapaume road near the site of the sugar factory that was captured on 15 September. There are three large cemeteries in the area, Courcelette British Cemetery, Regina Trench Cemetery and Adanac Cemetery.

THIEPVAL 1914-1915

British units began taking over from the French on the Somme in July-August 1915.

The French and Germans first clashed at Thiepval on 28 September 1914. This vital high ground overlooked the Ancre Valley and views across to Albert and the road to Amiens, as well as towards Grandcourt. The fighting for Thiepval, Authuille wood and Hill 141 lasted for a week before the focus of the fighting shifted north towards Arras during the phase of outflanking battles that became known as the Race to the Sea. The Württemberg regiments of the *26. Reserve-Division* remained in this sector facing the French regiments of the *22ème division d'infanterie* comprising of units

Pierre Marie Le Maitre of the 19éme Régiment d'infanterie was killed in action at Thiepval on 29 November 1914. He had recently learned that he was going to be a father. His wife never remarried and brought up their son alone.

raised in Brittany. After the ill-fated French attack of 17 December in the Authuille Wood and Ovillers sector, the trenches around Thiepval remained relatively quiet as each side dug in and strengthened their defences. The Germans built strong defensive redoubts at Hill 141 (Leipzig Salient) south of Thiepval and the Schwaben Redoubt just beyond the village cemetery to the north. Deep dugouts were built beneath the village and cellars were linked up, all but impervious except to the heaviest shells.

The British arrived in the sector at the end of July 1915, with Thiepval and Authuille being handed over to the 51st Highland Division where a special rapport was struck between the Bretons and Scots. The 8th Argyll and Sutherland Highlanders regimental piper, William Lawrie wrote a piece of music that was played as the Breton *116ème régiment d'infanterie* marched out of their billets and away from the Somme. The Scottish soldiers also inherited a dairy cow that enjoyed its own dugout in Thiepval Wood.

As the British build-up on the Somme continued, the sector became livelier as the Germans launched trench raids in order to ascertain which units now faced them. Trench raiding became a feature of the Thiepval sector, triggering nocturnal artillery duels where tens of thousands of shells could be fired by each side.

German artillery hidden in a barn, Thiepval 1914.

"They started bombarding us at 11 p.m., and kept it up until 12.30 a.m., and I don't think there has been anything worse for the time being in any part of the line. I should think we had 2,000 shells all about our little place.... We had to sit in our dug-out, with no help for ourselves and trust to luck." Private J. Hughes, 16th Lancashire Fusiliers. A German trench raid at Thiepval, 11 March 1916.

Thiepval château which was eventually reduced to rubble and brick dust.

THE FIGHTING OF 1916

The British bombardment preceding the offensive began on 24th June 1916 and the important sector of Thiepval was hit by 75,000 shells in one day. As the bombardment intensified, the Württembergers could only take to their deep dug-outs and pray that they would not be buried alive. The problem with the British artillery preparation was its lack of heavy guns, the bombardment caused miserable conditions for the Germans but their deep shelters in most places survived intact.

As elsewhere along the 14-mile attack frontage, lines of British infantry clambered out of their trenches at 7.30 a.m. on 1 July and began walking towards the German positions that were largely believed to have been battered into submission. The Germans of *RIR 99* emerged from their underground shelters and set up their machine-guns. The carnage began. Attacking the village directly and to the south around the Leipzig Salient, the men of the 32nd Division, the bulk of which were in the volunteer Pals Battalions, were systematically mown down. The only gains made were on Hill 141 south of the village which saw five British battalions severely mauled in the fight against men of *IR 180* for a gain of a few hundred metres of German defences. Losses for the 32nd were 3,949 and the reserve division, the 49th, lost 590 men.

"The 180th Regiment of Württembergers have withstood attacks on Thiepval for two years, but the 18th Division will take it tomorrow." Major-General Ivor Maxse, 18th (Eastern) Division.

A British infanryman of July 1916 with 1914 Pattern equipment and satchels for the PH gas helmet.

German MG 08 that caused so any of the casualties on 1 July. The mount of this machine-gun was captured at Thiepval on 26 September 1916.

Thiepval falls

A series of large-scale British, Commonwealth and French attacks further south had steadily, and at a terrible cost, pushed the German line back towards Bapaume and Péronne. Thiepval still stood like a rock in the German lines. The push along the Albert-Bapaume road and beyond Courcelette meant that the bastion could also be attacked from the rear. Attacking from the ground taken at Hill 141 had, in the space of two and half months, advanced the British line less than a mile.

The task fell to the 18th Division, under the command the innovative Major-General Ivor Maxse. Zero hour was set at 12.35 p.m. in order to allow enough daylight to consolidate and dig-in, as well as preventing the Germans from being able to organize counter-attacks. The attacking soldiers advanced behind a creeping barrage and by 2.30 p.m. had captured most of the ruined village, assisted in the task by tanks which were being used in action for the second time.

The following day saw the battle rage around the Schwaben Redoubt a few hundred yards beyond Thiepval and it was not until 12 October that this infamous strongpoint finally fell. The entire Thiepval crest was finally captured following a four-division attack on 21 October, capturing Stuff Trench and Regina Trench as far as the Pys to Courcelette road. The British now controlled the view over the German lines towards Grandcourt.

Thiepval was back in German hands in March 1918 and was re-captured within a day by the 17th (Northern) Division in late August.

« It was Geoffrey Salter speaking out firmly in the darkness. Stuff Trench – this was Stuff Trench; three-feet deep, corpses under foot, corpses on the parapet. He told us, while shell after shell slipped in crescendo wailing into the vibrating ground, that his brother had been killed, and that he had buried him..... » Lieutenant Edmund Blunden, 11th Royal Sussex Regt., 39th Division.

What to see

There are many memorials around the Thiepval sector. The imposing Thiepval Memorial to the Missing of the Somme battlefields bears the names of 72,194 officers and men of the United Kingdom and South African forces. These men died in the Somme battle sector before 20th March 1918 and have no known grave. There is an excellent visitors centre with knowledgeable staff and rest facilities. A short walk down the path through the fields will take you to the site of the Leipzig Salient, today a tree-filled quarry. Nearby is a memorial to the Dorsetshire Regt. whose 1st battalion suffered heavy losses here on 1 July. The Lonsdale Cemetery has 1,542 graves, including that of Sgt. James Turnbull who won the Victoria Cross on 1 July in the Leipzig Salient. Authuille Wood has many remains of trench lines running through it. The 18th Division's obelisk overlooks Thiepval Wood and is placed near the site of the former château. The site of the Schwaben Redoubt is not marked but it was in the fields opposite the large farm just beyond the small civilian cemetery on the road to Grandcourt. The nearby village of Authuille has many memorials, notably to the Salford, Glasgow and Newcastle Pals as well as Authuille Military and Blighty Valley Cemeteries.

Germans observing from the second defence line at Thiepval, 12 March 1916.

THE 36TH (ULSTER) DIVISION

Just to the west of Thiepval lies an imposing wood that marked the frontline here at the end of September 1914 when it was held by Breton troops. The forwards trenches ran along its edge as the road dips down to the river Ancre, and along its eastern edge and in the fields just beyond facing the German defences in the château park. Today the area is known for the sacrifice of the 36th (Ulster) Division who attacked from the wood and across the valley on 1 July 1916.

The Division was a New Army formation raised with volunteers from the pre-war Ulster Volunteer Force; it arrived in France in October 1915.

The 36th Division plan was to reach the Schwaben Redoubt and the intermediate positions of the Hansa Line, with the 32nd Division, on their right flank, taking Thiepval itself. The ambitious plan foresaw the Ulstermen advancing north through Stuff Redoubt before reaching Grandcourt. Facing the Division were the Württembergers of *RIR 99*, men who had held this ground since September 1914. The attack, helped by a smokescreen, broke through the German defences, battered by a week-long artillery and trench mortar bombardment. However, with the Salford Pals' attack having been annihilated by machine-gun fire, the Germans were able to bring down fire on the Ulstermen

A German soldier in a trench at Thiepval, early 1916.

14

as they advanced towards the Schwaben Redoubt. The men who had reached the redoubt were effectively cut-off and German machine-gun and artillery fire prevented any reinforcements reaching them. Fresh German troops were brought forward from Grandcourt and began a counter-attack against the brave Ulstermen.

The gallant survivors were finally driven back by a counter-attack at 10 p.m. The 36th (Ulster) Division's losses were 216 officers and 5,266 men.

"I am holding the end of a communication trench in A line with a few bombers and a Lewis Gun. We cannot hold on much longer. We are being pressed on all sides and ammunition is almost finished." A message sent back by Captain Davidson of the 13th Royal Irish Rifles, killed in action, 1 July 1916.

Surrendering Württembergers of *RIR 99* make their way back to the British front-line at Thiepval Wood. "Enemy prisoners now began to come in.....They seemed for the most part dazed and bewildered by the fury of our bombardment and were only too glad to surrender....The first batches of these prisoners were so anxious to reach the shelter of our trenches that they outstripped their escort and....were bayonetted by our reinforcements." 10th Royal Inniskilling Fusiliers (Derry Volunteers) battle report..

What to see

Thiepval Wood is now owned by the Somme Association based in Northern Ireland. Excellent guided tours of the excavated frontline trenches are run by from the Ulster Tower. The Ulster Tower stands as a Memorial to the 36th (Ulster) Division and stands close to the German frontline. It was inaugurated in November 1921 and is a close replica of Helen's Tower in the grounds of the Clandeboye Estate in County Down where many men of the 36th Division trained prior to leaving for France. The small visitor's centre is an excellent refreshments stop and its small museum is full of fascinating artefacts found in and around Thiepval Wood. A little further down a track along the road to the Ancre is the remains of a German machine-gun emplacement known as the Pope's Nose. Many of the Ulstermen lie in the nearby Connaught and Mill Road Cemeteries.

French soldiers in Auchonvillers in early 1915. They wear steel skullcaps that were used before the introduction of helmets.

NEWFOUNDLAND PARK

The frontline dropped down to the valley through which the river Ancre runs, with the village of Hamel just in front of the marshy area known to the Germans as the Beaver Colony, before climbing up the steep hill towards Auchonvillers. The area known today as Newfoundland Park is one of the best preserved battlefields of the Western Front.

The area was first fought over on 6 October 1914 as the German *2. Garde-Infanterie-Division* made a fresh push between Achiet-le-Petit, Puisieux and Serre. *RIR 99*, *IR 110* and the Bavarian *IR 17* came up against staunch resistance from territorial troops and elements of the *21ème division d'infanterie*.

The British took over the sector in July 1915. This sector of frontline was allocated to the 29th Division for the opening day of the Somme offensive. The Division was formed in early 1915 with Regular Army battalions that had returned from far-flung corners of the Empire, having been replaced there by territorial units. The 29th Division also received a few New Army battalions and first saw action at Gallipoli between April 1915 and January 1916 before arriving in France in March. The 29th held the trenches in this sector for the next three months and began preparing for the coming offensive. As elsewhere, the Germans were subjected to an intense week-long artillery bombardment ; an hour before Zero Hour, trench mortars joined in and at 7.20 a.m. a huge mine was blown in front of the

The Caribou monument in the early 1930s.

village of Beaumont-Hamel. The story here was the same as in most other parts of the line on Saturday 1 July. The men clambered out of their trenches and were met with a hail of machine-gun and artillery fire. The 1st Newfoundland Regiment (honoured with the Royal prefix in 1918), was formed with volunteers from the dominion in August-September 1914, mostly from the fishing communities and St. John's. The first waves had gone over but problems in communications meant that their fate was unknown. This was compounded by white flares being seen, the signal that the first objective had been captured, but was also that used by German artillery when their own fire was falling short. The Newfoundlanders, along with the 1st Essex, were ordered to attack. The Regiment began its advance at 9.15 a.m., they had to cross in the open towards their own front line and as soon as they crested the brow of the ridge were cut down by enemy fire. Some groups of men managed to get through the gaps in the wire and even as far as the German frontline but the attack was over within half an hour. The Newfoundlanders suffered losses of 658 out of the estimated 780 men who went into the attack (every regiment left behind 10% of its men before an attack). Losses for the 29th Division were 5,240 officers and men.

The trenches at Newfoundland Park today.

The area was successfully attacked on 13 November 1916 by the 51st (Highland) Division, resulting in the capture of Beaumont-Hamel. The war returned here in March 1918 and this part of the frontline is visible in the park today. A large-scale trench raid was undertaken by the 17th (Northern) Division in May 1918, resulting in the capture of many prisoners and guns.

"I Kept my eye on the officer just ahead. He turned to wave us on and then down he went – just as though he was bloody pole-axed. I just kept moving. I wasn't really thinking straight....And there were blokes just laying everywhere." Private Charlie Byrne, 2nd Hampshires, Vickers MG team, attached to the 1st Newfoundland Regiment.

What to see

Newfoundland Park was purchased by the Dominion's government after the war. Today it is run by the Canadian government with Canadian guides. There is an excellent visitors centre and maps are available for self-guided tours of the many trench lines, memorials and cemeteries within the boundaries of the park. The village of Auchonvillers is a kilometre away and the "Ocean Villas" tea rooms provide refreshments. There is also an excavated communications trench there that can be seen although it is best to arrange this prior to any visit. There is also a private museum covering both world wars.

French soldiers in a frontline trench listening post in front of Beaumont-Hamel, late 1914.

BEAUMONT-HAMEL

The village of Beaumont-Hamel lies just beyond the boundaries of Newfoundland Park. It was captured by the Germans in October 1914 and was attacked by the French *65ème régiment d'infanterie* in November 1914. The village was a first day objective on 1 July and the German defenders of *IR 119* were attacked by the 4th Division to the north across the Redan Ridge and the 29th Division.

The Hawthorn Ridge mine

It was on the high ground in front of the village that a huge mine was blown ten minutes before Zero Hour. The mine was designed to remove a German redoubt that protruded from their frontline. The task of digging the mine fell to the 252nd Tunnelling Company who had been allocated the Hébuterne – Beaumont-

Hamel sector. When the tunnel was completed it was 910 metres long and 17 deep. The chamber was filled with 18,000 kgs of ammonal explosive. The decision was made to blow the mine ten minutes before the attack ; initially, the VIII Corps commander, Lt.Gen. Aylmet Hunter-Weston, wanted to blow the mine four hours before, allowing the crater to be occupied and consolidated. However, at 4th Army, it was considered that the British did not have a very good track record of occupying mine craters and thus the unsatisfactory compromise to blow ten minutes before was reached.

The mine explosion was filmed by British cinematographer Geoffrey Malins from a distance of around 800 metres.

The explosion was followed by an assault launched by two British battalions but this was soon repulsed by the German defenders of *IR 119*, shaken but unbroken by the enormous explosion. The main assault went in at 7.30 a.m. but followed the same sad pattern as elsewhere. German defences were intact, hidden artillery positions sprung to life and the skilled machine-gun teams began reaping their grim harvest.

Beaumont-Hamel eventually fell on 13 November 1916 to the 51st (Highland) Division. The weather before the attack had been atrocious and the Scots advanced across a shell-torn morass. At 5.45 a.m. a second mine was blown using the old tunnel of 1 July. This signalled the attack, there had been no preliminary barrage in order to maintain the element of surprise. The village and the objectives beyond it were taken by nightfall but fighting continued in the sector until the close of the offensive on 18 November.

"Visibility was good. The sun could be seen reflecting on English bayonets. Their columns advancing down from Auchonvillers, carrying bridges and wooden planks with them to cross our trenches with.....the 10th and 11th companies greeted them with a withering hail of machine-gun and rifle fire, effectively stalling the attack." Regimental history, IR 119.

The ruins of Beaumont-Hamel in November 1916.

The explosion of the Hawthorn Ridge mine "The ground where I stood gave a mighty convulsion. It rocked and swayed. I gripped hold of my tripod to steady myself. Then for all the world like a gigantic sponge, the earth rose high in the air to the height of hundreds of feet. Higher and higher it rose, and with a horrible grinding roar the earth settles back upon itself, leaving in its place a mountain of smoke." — Geoffrey Malins

What to see

A good start to a visit of this area is at the entrance to the sunken lane next to the memorial to the 8th Argyll and Sutherland Highlanders. The sunken lane that climbs up towards the Redan Ridge is hallowed ground for many Somme battlefield pilgrims as it was here that Malins filmed anxious men of the 1st Lancashire Fusiliers shortly before they went over the top and, in many cases, to their deaths. The ring of trees on the high ground in front of the village marks the double craters of the Hawthorn Ridge mines. They can be visited but the climb can be slippery and treacherous. Inside the village is the flagpole memorial to the 51st (Highland) Division.

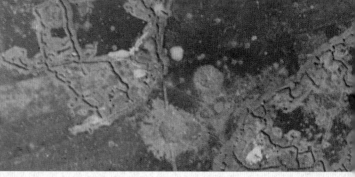

A French aerial photo showing attack preparations the day before the 7 June attack on Serre. The German trenches are to the right. The road is today's D919 between Mailly-Maillet and Puisieux.

The Redan Ridge craters, 6 June 1915. The French trenches are to the left. This sector was taken over by the British two months later.

SERRE AND THE REDAN RIDGE

From Beaumont-Hamel, the old frontline stretches across the Redan Ridge towards the German held village of Serre. A good view of this part of the battlefield can be had from the Hawthorn Ridge crater with the Cross of Sacrifice in the numerous British cemeteries marking where the tide of battle ebbed and flowed.

The ridge was fought over in October 1914 as the Germans sought once more to outflank the French territorial units and those of the *21ème division d'infanterie*. The top of the ridge also saw mining activity although the craters have now been mostly filled in. Apart from the line of cemeteries there is little to show that the Western Front stretched across this wind-swept part of the Somme. It was attacked by the 4th Division on 1 July but no gains were made here and the Division lost 3,600 officers and men.

The French attack at Hébuterne June 1915

On 7 June, the French *65ème*, *93ème* and *137ème régiments d'infanterie* attacked 1,800 metres of German frontline, capturing two trench lines. The following day, the *14ème* and *75ème R.I.* attacked just north of the newly-captured positions, then again, south of La Signy farm on 9 June with the *233ème*, *243ème* and *327ème R.I.* The Germans launched a ferocious counter-attack on the 12th but were beaten off. A final French attack was launched on the 13th, capturing Toutvent Farm but not the village of Serre. It was here that the frontline settled up to the battles of 1916. French losses between 7 – 13 June were 11,000.

The village of Serre sits upon a ridge that dominates the ground towards Mailly-Maillet and Puisieux. The task of capturing it fell to the 4th Division attacking across the Redan Ridge with the German Heidenkopf redoubt on their left flank, assisted here by the 1/6th and 1/8th Royal Warwicks detached from the reserve 48th Division. The Heidenkopf was penetrated but the position was finally abandoned the following day.

Two German RIR 121 men bringing up rations. One of the trench signs is marked Serre.

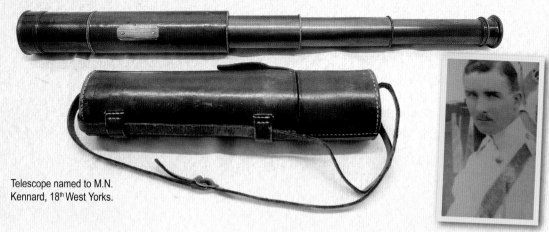

Telescope named to M.N. Kennard, 18th West Yorks.

Maurice Nicholl Kennard before the war.

The 31st Division was tasked with the assault on the village of Serre itself. The Division was formed in April 1915 and comprised of many Pals battalions raised in Yorkshire and Lancashire towns such as Sheffield, Barnsley, Accrington, Hull, Leeds and Bradford. The attack waves passed through gaps made in the British wire at 7.20 a.m. and lay down in No Man's Land. The 15th West Yorks (1st Leeds Pals) were stopped by machine-gun fire, the 16th West Yorks (1st Bradford Pals) were also wiped out by concentrated fire. The 11th East Lancs (Accrington Pals) and 12th York & Lancs (Sheffield City) were cut down by fire from the left flank. The Hull Pals battalions of the East Yorkshire Regiment were also stopped and the attack was suspended. Losses to the division were 3,600 for no gain.

A further attack was launched against Serre on 13 November 1916 by the 3rd Division. The attack broke down due to the muddy conditions and exhaustion of the men who had had to march up to nine miles before the attack, laden down with up to 30 kg of equipment. The 31st Division was back here too the same day, providing a defensive flank for the 3rd Division. Serre was finally occupied in late February 1917 as the Germans withdrew from the Somme battlefields to their new positions along the Hindenburg Line. War returned to this shattered land in March 1918.

Before the war, Maurice Nicholl Kennard was a captain with the 6th Dragoon Guards. He was wounded near Messines in October 1914. He was posted to the 18th West Yorks (2nd Bradford Pals) in April 1916. The Battalion was in the third wave of the attack and were hit by machine-gun fire coming from the Heidenkopf to their right, as well as artillery fire. Most of the casualties occurred before they reached their own wire. "*It was hell on earth. Everyone dropped flat on their stomachs. Colonel Kennard was standing and only carrying a walking stick. He called out, "Come on boys, up you get" and began to walk towards the enemy.*" Private Frank Burn, 2nd Bradford Pals. Kennard, 32, was never found and his name appears on the Thiepval Memorial.

"**The name of Serre and the date of 1st July is engraved deep in our hearts, along with the faces of our 'Pals', a grand crowd of chaps. We were two years in the making and ten minutes in the destroying.**" (**Private A.V. Pearson, Leeds Pals**)

18th West Yorks shoulder title found at Bus-les-Artois where the 2nd Bradford Pals were billeted before leaving for the trenches.

Fricourt station, just behind French lines.

FRICOURT-MAMETZ

The next part of this guide book will once again allow the battlefield visitor to start from the town of Albert. Fricourt and Mametz were fortified German villages that both fell in the opening stages of the 1916 offensive.

Fricourt was the scene of fierce fighting on 28 September 1914 as French forces tried to stem the German advance towards Albert. A night attack was launched by elements of *IR 111*, *RIR 40* and *Reserve Jäger Bn. 8* but was broken by heavy fire from Fricourt itself and the hills around it. The Germans pressed the attack the following day but the French had already pulled out of Fricourt and dug in on the hills beyond it. The focus of the German attack was now on Hill 110 south of Fricourt and which overlooked Mametz. The men of *RIR 111* and *RIR 40* scaled the hill in the face of heavy fire and despite terrible losses held on to the crest. The French counter-attacked but the Germans held on and the lines settled here and on the high ground to the north of Fricourt. The French made a final attack on the village in October but this too failed and the Germans began fortifying the village and linking up the cellars. By November, both sides began mining activity on Hill 110 and the Tambour sector facing the village. 17 December saw a number of French attacks. Mametz fell to men of the *236ème R.I.* but they were forced out after a counter-attack and hand-to-hand fighting. Hill 110 was also the scene of a brief truce on Christmas Day 1914 between men of the *205ème R.I.* and *RIR 109*.

The British arrived in the sector in July 1915 and the 174th Tunnelling Company took over the Tambour and Hill 110 mines. The attack on Fricourt fell to the 21st Division and the 50th Brigade of the 17th (Northern) Division. Mametz lay in the path of 7th Division. Unlike further north, there was success here. Both villages fell; Mametz during the day and with Fricourt being evacuated by the Germans during the night due to the advance on either side of the village. This came at a price however; the 21st Division lost 4,256 men, the 50th Brigade 1,155 and the 7th Division 3,380. The 10th West Yorks had the heaviest battalion losses on 1 July with 733 casualties.

"I am looking at a sunlit picture of hell."
Siegfried Sassoon, 1st Royal Welch Fusiliers, Mametz 1 July 1916.

The mine craters on Hill 110 (Bois Français) in May 1915. The first French mine at Fricourt was blown on 19 March 1915.

The German lines seen from the frontline in front of Fricourt. To the right are the German trenches leading up to Hill 110.

What to see

The area has many traces of the war. Trench lines and craters can still be seen on Hill 110 and in the Tambour in front of Fricourt. There are many cemeteries in the Fricourt-Mametz area, including the villages of Becordel-Becourt. Fricourt British Cemetery has a memorial to the 7th Green Howards. Fricourt New Military Cemetery lies on the ground where the 10th West Yorks were wiped out and looks across the Tambour mine crater field. Fricourt German Cemetery contains the remains of more than 17,000 men. The church holds a memorial plaque to the 17th (Northern) Division. The road up to Point 110 military cemeteries takes you to the Bois Français sector and mine craters are still visible here. Mametz has three British cemeteries, that of Dantzig Alley lies on the outskirts of the village and Gordon Cemetery lies on the Péronne road. A little further along is the Devonshire Cemetery where men of the 9th and 8th Devons were buried in a frontline trench in the days after the attack. There is a small memorial plaque to the Manchester and Oldham Pals in the village and a 38th (Welsh) Division plaque in the church.

THE WOODS

High Wood in August 1916

Mametz Wood, Bazentin Woods, High Wood, Delville Wood, Bernafay and Trones Wood would become headline names during the fighting of 1916. Today they still bear traces of the terrible events that took place there, with trench lines running through the still visible craters. All of these woods can be seen from a high point at Montauban on the Bazentin-le-Grand road.

Bernafay Wood fell relatively easily to the 9th (Scottish) Division but Trones Wood proved to be a more formidable obstacle as the Germans reinforced it. It was fought over between 8 – 14 July and was finally cleared by the 18th (Eastern) Division on the right flank of the Bazentin Ridge attack. A memorial to the 18th Division is on the edge of the wood on the road to Guillemont. Just beyond the wood is where the frontline remained for two months.

A rare photo taken from German positions in High Wood.

Mametz Wood is a large, dense wood that was fought over by the 38th (Welsh) Division, first on 7 July, then on the 10th. After two days of intense fighting, the Welsh soldiers cleared the shattered wood but at the cost of almost 4,000 casualties. Today, a magnificent dragon memorial looks over the edge of the wood. The memorial is accessible via a track from Mametz which was known as Death Valley and a main route to the frontline during the fighting at High Wood.

High Wood lies on a ridge that afforded good views across the German rear area towards Bapaume. The fighting here was amongst the most intense of the summer battles. It was reached on 14th July after the successful night-time Bazentin Ridge assault but the opportunity of capturing it was lost due to a lack of reserves and also bad communication. The area to the right of the wood also saw a cavalry attack but this was stopped and the fighting soon settled into the same pattern of attrition. The wood saw two months of constant fighting. There are many memorials to the

British regiments which fought here. On the south-eastern edge is a memorial to the Cameron Highlanders and Black Watch, nearby is the crater of a mine blown under a German machine-gun strongpoint. On the roadside are memorials to the 47th (London) Division and Glasgow Highlanders.
*Delville Wood will be covered on the page concerning Longueval.

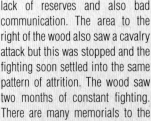

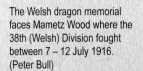
The Welsh dragon memorial faces Mametz Wood where the 38th (Welsh) Division fought between 7 – 12 July 1916.
(Peter Bull)

British bullets found on the edge of High Wood.

A gas attack in the Montauban-Carnoy sector, launched by the 18th (Eastern) Division, June 1916.

A Livens flame projector of the type used at Casino Point north of Carnoy, 1 July 1916.

CARNOY- MONTAUBAN

1914

War came to the quiet villages of Montauban and Carnoy as early as 28 August 1914 as the Germans swept through the area in their advance to Amiens. Following the Battle of the Marne, the Germans pulled out on 11 September but were back again on the 28th during the series of outflanking battles that eventually took the fighting towards the North Sea. The French *69ème R.I.* suffered heavy losses defending the ridge here on 28 September 1914 against the Bavarian *RIR 5* and there was hand-to-hand fighting in Montauban which eventually fell to the Bavarians, whereas Carnoy remained in French hands. As in other sectors of the Somme, Montauban was the subject of a heavy attack on 17 December 1914.

1916

The attack on the Montauban-Carnoy area fell to the 18th (Eastern) Division and the 30th Division. This artillery preparation was also supported by French heavy artillery in this sector, something that would play a fundamental role in the successful penetration of the German lines. At Casino Point north of Carnoy, the 183rd Tunnelling Company blew two mines, albeit much smaller ones than at La Boisselle. An underground flamethrower was also used, breaking the overhead cover just before the assault and spraying the Germans with liquid fire. The area is also famous for Captain Nevill of the 8th East Surreys who went over the top with the men of his company kicking footballs in order to take their minds off the ordeal. He was subsequently killed and is buried in nearby Carnoy Military Cemetery. The 30th Division was to the right and was tasked with taking the village of Montauban which was entered at 10.05 a.m. by men of the Manchesters and Royal Scots Fusiliers. The advance of these two divisions in this sector and the taking of their objectives would shape the strategy of the Somme offensive over the next few months. Success came at a price however; the 18th Division suffered 3,115 casualties and the 30th Division 3,011. Germans losses here were the heaviest on 1 July with RIR 109 losing 2,147 men and Bavarian RIR 6, 1,810.

The area was recaptured by the Germans in March 1918 and retaken by the 18th (Eastern) Division in August.

A British PH gas helmet used in the Somme battles of 1916.

A German soldier in Montauban, 1915.

What to see

Montauban has a memorial to the 30th Division Liverpool and Manchester Pals. On the road to Guillemont stands a memorial cross to *Capitaine* Henri Thieron de Monclin and the *69ème régiment d'infanterie* who made a brave stand here on 28 September 1914 in order to cover the withdrawal of another French unit as they fell back towards Fricourt. Quarry Cemetery on the road to Bazentin-le-Grand has 740 Commonwealth graves. Carnoy Military Cemetery has 854 graves. Captain Nevill's grave is number 28, row E.

MARICOURT – HARDECOURT-AUX-BOIS

Maricourt was the junction of the French and British armies. Maricourt saw extremely heavy fighting during three days at the end of September 1914. Following the allied victory on the Marne in early September, Crown Prince Rupprecht of Bavaria was ordered by Falkenhayn to move the *6.Armee* north and begin what the Germans called the race for the flank, a series of attacks that have passed into posterity as the Race to the Sea. The initial fighting began further south of the river Somme in Chaulnes, Lihons, Foucaucourt and Dompierre as the Bavarian *1.Korps* ran into advancing French territorial units, thus halting any advance by either side south of the river. The next German thrust was made by the Bavarian *2.Korps* against Albert, then Amiens, with the *XIV. Reserve-Korps* advancing from Cambrai down the Bapaume-Albert road.

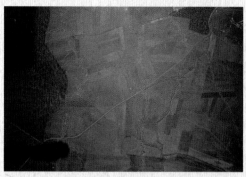

French lines in front of Favière wood near Maricourt and German lines (to the right), 26 March 1915. The almost total lack of artillery fire damage shows that this was a quiet sector at the time.

Maricourt lay astride a vital position on the crossroads of the Péronne-Albert and Suzanne-Longueval roads with the high ground dominating the surrounding area. On 27 September 1914, the German *18. Infanterie-Regiment* suffered terrible casualties attacking the village from Bois Favière near Hardecourt. Further attempts to capture the village were made, but after 29 September the French had brought further reinforcements to the area and it remained in French hands with the German lines sweeping around Montauban, before heading south in front of Hardecourt-aux-Bois.

German troops at rest behind the lines.

What to see

There is a small memorial and explanation tablet on the Maricourt-Montauban road marking the junction between the 17th Bn. The King's Regiment (Liverpool) and the French *153ème régiment d'infanterie*. A kilometre beyond the village is a memorial to the *224ème régiment d'infanterie* who fought here on 17 December 1914. Péronne Road Cemetery has 1,348 graves. The church in Hardecourt-aux-Bois has memorial tablets to French soldiers who fell around the village. The road towards Guillemont has a memorial cross to Capitaine Augustin Cochin of the 146ème R.I. who fell there on 8 July. Following the road to the left of the cross, one will come to a large cross marking the emplacement of Maltzhorn Farm which was the focus of heavy fighting in July. Nearby is a memorial to Marcel Boucher and Roméo Lepage of the *153ème R.I.*, both killed there on 28 July.

At the junction of the British and French armies were the 17th Bn. The King's Regiment (Liverpool) and the *French 153ème régiment d'infanterie*, which had already been in action at the battle of Verdun. Lieutenant-Colonel Fairfax and commandant Petit of these two units, linked arms and advanced together on 1 July. The advance here was a success, but Hardecourt-aux-Bois held out for another week, with the frontline then settling to the north and east of the village for a further two months.

L'ACTUALITÉ par la Carte postale :
L'OFFENSIVE FRANÇAISE ET ANGLAISE DANS LA SOMME
RECENT events in Postal Cards : The British and French offensive on the Somme.

GUILLEMONT

The village of Guillemont was at the heart of the fighting in the summer of 1916. However, the first fighting took place here on 28 August 1914 as the French *265ème régiment d'infanterie* from Nantes tried to hold back elements of the German *IV. Reserve-Korps*. Fighting returned to this area once more on 28 September 1914.

Once the frontlines had settled, Guillemont became a quiet village in the German rear area and was largely untroubled by war. All that would change when the frontline settled in front of the area in mid-July 1916.
The capture of Trones Wood on 14 July and the French push just south of the wood brought the frontline to the fields in front of the village. The frontline would remain there for the next six weeks despite constant British attacks. Nearby Waterlot Farm on the Longueval road was captured by the 35th Division on 17 July. The next big push on the village was on the 23rd by the 30th Division, supported by the 3rd Division attacking south of Longueval. The attack was a total failure and losses were heavy. Further costly attacks were made on 8 and 18 August but the crater field where the village once stood was at last captured on 3 September by the 20th Light Division.

The steeple of Guillemont church was blown up by the Germans late 1914 to prevent the French from using it as an artillery marker.

Ernst Jünger and Fusilier Regiment 73. arrived in the Guillemont sector on 24 August 1916. In Jünger's famous war memoir, Storm of Steel, he gives a glimpse of the horrors of holding the line against British attacks at Guillemont.

There is a road named after Ernst Jünger in Guillemont.

The sunken road at Guillemont in August 1916.

"The sunken road and the ground behind was full of German dead; the ground in front of English. Arms, legs, and heads stuck out stark above the lips of the craters. In front of our miserable defences there were torn-off limbs and corpses over many of which cloaks and ground-sheets had been thrown to hide the fixed stare of their distorted features. In spite of the heat no one thought for a moment of covering them with soil." Ernst Jünger, Storm of Steel.

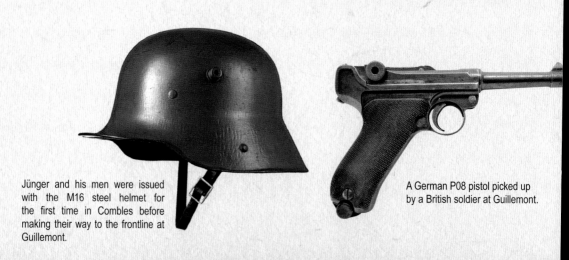

Jünger and his men were issued with the M16 steel helmet for the first time in Combles before making their way to the frontline at Guillemont.

A German P08 pistol picked up by a British soldier at Guillemont.

What to see

Approaching from Montauban, the ground in front of Trones Wood is where the frontline passed between 14 July and 3 September ; over to the left is a grain silo where Waterlot Farm once stood, with the mass of Delville Wood behind it. Guillemont Road Cemetery has 2,263 Commonwealth graves, including that of Raymond Asquith, the British Prime Minister's son who was mortally wounded nearby at Ginchy. The village itself has a memorial to the 16th (Irish) Division. Entrances to German dugouts can be seen in Rue d'en Haut. On the Combles road are memorials to the 20th (Light) Division and the men of the French 265ème régiment d'infanterie who fell between Ginchy and Guillemont on 28 August 1914. Near the site of Waterlot Farm is a small memorial to Lieutenant Marsden-Smedley whose body, like so many others, was never found.

The wood today still bears witness to the fighting of 1916.

LONGUEVAL AND DELVILLE WOOD

As in most of the surrounding towns and villages, war swept through the small village of Longueval in August, then September 1914.

The frontline reached the village on 14 July 1916 following the successful attack on Bazentin Ridge. The Germans reacted quickly and brought up reinforcements to the large Bois d' Elville on the eastern edge of the village. The 1st South African Brigade of the 9th (Scottish) Division advanced into the wood at 5 a.m. on 15 July, capturing all but the north-west corner. The German 24. Reserve-Division rushed up reinforcements but their two counter-attacks made little progress. When night fell, the wood was saturated by artillery fire and gas shells before the Germans made further counter-attacks. On the 16th, the South Africans attempted to capture the north-west corner of the wood but were repulsed, falling back to the middle of the wood and subjected to heavy artillery fire for the rest of the day.

This illustration captures some of the ferocity of the hand-to-hand fighting that took place within Delville Wood.

"Delville Wood had disintegrated into a shattered wasteland of shattered trees, charred and burning stumps, craters thick with mud and blood, and corpses, corpses everywhere. In places they were piled four deep. Worst of all was the lowing of the wounded. It sounded like a cattle ring at the spring fair."
A German officer in Delville Wood.

The shattered remains of Delville Wood in September 1916.

The following day saw attacks by both sides with a large German attack being made mid-afternoon from the east, north and north-west. On the 18th, the South Africans received some reinforcements from the 3rd Division but came under a huge attack by over 6,000 German infantry from the north and north-east. There was close-quarter fighting all over the wood as isolated pockets of South Africans held on desperately. By now they were low, and in some cases, out of ammunition, they had no food or water and it was impossible to remove the wounded.

The survivors of the 1st South African Brigade were reached at last by troops of the 3rd Division on 20 July.

On 14 July, the 1st South African Brigade comprised of 123 officers and 3,032 other ranks. Six days later, this number stood at just under 800 officers and men.

Heavy fighting continued around Longueval and in Delville Wood throughout the summer with the British and Germans throwing division after division into the sector from High Wood, to the north-west, Longueval and Guillemont to the south-east. The wood was not cleared until 3 September, the day on which Guillemont also fell.

What to see

Today Delville Wood is the property of South Africa and is home to its national memorial. It was inaugurated in 1926 and also has a commemorative museum which was opened in 1986. The wood still bears the traces of the battle with shells craters and trench lines. There is an obelisk marking the emplacement of the South African Brigade's headquarters during their heroic stand in the wood. Opposite the wood is Delville Wood Cemetery containing 5,523 graves. In Longueval there is a piper's memorial and another to the 17th and 28th Battalion of the Middlesex Regiment. Caterpillar Valley Cemetery has 5,568 graves and on its eastern side, the New Zealand Memorial to the 1,200 New Zealand men who fell during the Battle of the Somme and who have no known grave. The New Zealand Division memorial is on the crest between High Wood and Delville Wood. The Division attacked across this area on 15 September.

CONTALMAISON

The small village of Contalmaison is five kilometres north-east of Albert and a kilometre and a half south of Pozières. It was a 1 July objective for the 34th Division attacking from La Boisselle and although some men managed to fight their way into the village, they were cut off and killed or captured. The Germans put up a dogged defence and the village did not fall until 10 July following sustained and costly attacks by the 7th, 17th (Northern) and 23rd Division. The capture of the village was essential to following operations at Pozières and Mametz Wood.

German troops in frontline trenches, Contalmaison, 5 July 1916. Note the Mauser G98 rifle with 25-round "trench" magazine.

McCrae's Battalion

This was the name given to the 16th (Service) Battalion Royal Scots. It was named after its founder, Sir George McCrae, a Scottish textile merchant and politician who raised the battalion in November 1914 and became its colonel. The Battalion comprised of volunteers from Edinburgh who answered Lord Kitchener's call to arms. It was the first of what became known as footballer's battalions as it was formed around the Heart of Midlothian football club that was top of the Scottish league in 1914. Sixteen Heart's players enlisted, followed by 500 supporters, as well as players and supporters of other clubs. Part of the 34th Division, some men of McCrae's Battalion succeeded in breaking through the Germans lines and reached Contalmaison where they were cut off and eventually killed or captured. The Battalion lost 75% of its men on 1 July.

Men of McCrae's Battalion at camp in Great Britain before leaving for France. "...I see the faces of my boys. So young and full of promise. The sorrow and the pride are overwhelming. Sorrow at the loss and pride in the manner of their dying. They never flinched. Faced by a veritable storm of shot and shell, they marched towards the guns beside their friends." Extract from a letter written by Sir George McCrae in 1928 to a former member of his battalion.

What to see

Next to the church in Contalmaison is the 15th and 16th Royal Scots Memorial cairn inaugurated in 2004. Nearby is a memorial to Lt. Donald Bell V.C. of the 9th Yorkshires who was killed there on 10 July 1916. He was the first British professional footballer to voluntarily enlist. He was awarded the Victoria Cross for his action in capturing a German machine-gun on 5 July and was killed whilst attempting a similar feat on the ground where the memorial stands. He is buried at nearby Gordon Dump Cemetery. At the rear of the civilian cemetery is a memorial to the 12th Manchesters overlooking the edge of Mametz Wood where they lost many men in the Quadrangle trenches on the edge of the wood, along with other units of the 17th (Northern) Division. Peake Wood Cemetery has 101 graves and nearby is a small private memorial to Captain Francis Dodgson who was killed there on 10 July. Contalmaison Chateau Cemetery has 292 burials.

Combles high street in the summer of 1916.

COMBLES

The large village of Combles lies in a valley dominated by Leuze and Bouleaux Woods to the north-east and the high ground leading up to Rancourt in the west. It was in German hands in late August 1914 then briefly relinquished before remaining under German occupation until 25 September 1916. During the fighting in the French sector of Maurepas and the British at Guillemont, it was a main axis for arriving German reinforcements and was, therefore, the focus of heavy allied artillery bombardment.

Before Combles was evacuated by the Germans, there had been very heavy fighting to the east at Falfemont Farm where the 5th Division attacked on 3 September with the French on their right flank, but the farm did not fall until the 5th. Next in the line was the 56th (London)

Division fighting through Leuze and Bouleaux woods on the high ground above Combles. This division found itself on the extreme right of the huge attack of 15th September, the left flank of which was at Thiepval. This attack is famous for being the day on which tanks were used for the first time. Combles eventually fell on the day of the next large-scale attack on 26 September. The 56th Division pushed through Bouleaux Wood to the north-west and the French *110ème and 73ème R.I.* to the south-east forcing the Germans to pull out of Combles before the allies linked up beyond the village.

What to see

There is a concrete German observation bunker on the south-west edge of Leuze Wood, overlooking the valley and Falfemont Farm sector fought over in early September. This was also close to where the two tanks began moving in the 15 September attack. Bouleaux Wood is on the other side of the Combles-Guillemont road. Guards Cemetery contains 186 burials and Combles Cemetery Extension has 1,508 graves, including Corporal Pattinson who was a crew member of tank C 14. When the tank became stuck in a shell-hole its crew members tried to dig it out. The tank came under attack by German bombers and Pattinson was killed attempting to throw a German grenade back at the attackers. On the site of the old Falfemont Farm is a battlefield grave to three British soldiers.

2nd Lt. Purdy's C16 seen several weeks after the fall of Combles.

The tanks at Combles

Three tanks were allocated to the 56th Division's part in the attack, C16 commanded by 2nd Lt. Purdy, C13 by Lt. Sir John Dashwood and C14 by 2nd Lt. Arnold. C16 and C14 were 'female' tanks, that is to say armed with machine-guns rather than 6-pounder guns. The tanks left their starting point in Chimpanzee Valley the day before the attack, an area just over three kilometres from their jumping off positions near Leuze Wood. However, this approach brought them across the shattered battlefields and progress was slow. Near the Hardecourt-Guillemont road, taped lanes took the three tanks towards their positions. They were guided by Rifleman Gray of the 9th London Regiment. Dashwood's tank broke a track near Angle wood in front of the shattered ruins of Falfemont Farm and was rendered useless. The two remaining tanks carried on, still guided by Gray, the noise of their tracks and engines masked by artillery fire. C14 started on the western side of Leuze Wood, crossed the Combles-Guillemont road and proceeded to attack German positions near Bouleaux Wood. C14 eventually became stuck in shell-hole and was abandoned by its crew at 4 p.m.

C16 advanced along the southern edge of Leuze Wood and advanced towards the orchard close to where a modern water tower stands today. The tank then turned back towards the wood and was hit by artillery, possibly British, losing a track and becoming immobilised. Its crew used the machine-guns to fend off German attacks.

2nd Lt. Purdy, commander of tank C16.

GINCHY – LESBOEUFS – FLERS – GUEDECOURT

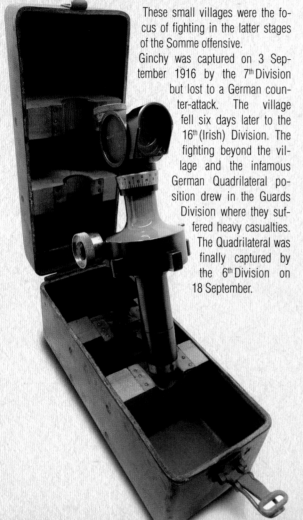

These small villages were the focus of fighting in the latter stages of the Somme offensive.

Ginchy was captured on 3 September 1916 by the 7th Division but lost to a German counter-attack. The village fell six days later to the 16th (Irish) Division. The fighting beyond the village and the infamous German Quadrilateral position drew in the Guards Division where they suffered heavy casualties. The Quadrilateral was finally captured by the 6th Division on 18 September.

Lesboeufs is a short distance from Ginchy and was captured by the 6th and Guards Divisions on 25 September 1916. It was recaptured on 24 March 1918 during the German spring offensive and was the scene of a fierce rear-guard action by the 63rd Royal Naval Division's machine-gun battalion.

Flers was the scene of fighting on 26 September 1914. The area around Flers was attacked by three divisions on 15 September 1916. One of the tanks allocated to the attack, D17, commanded by 2nd Lt. Hastie, pushed on up the main street of Flers accompanied by men of the 41st Division.

Guedecourt was attacked by the New Zealand, 55th and 21st Divisions on 25 September 1916. The line was then pushed forward towards the ridge beyond the village during the Transloy Ridge battles in October. The fighting continued in this sector between Le Sars and Morval. The area was held by the Australians from the end of October and throughout the winter of 1916-17.

This German artillery gun sight was found at Bulls Road, Flers on 15 September 1916.

What to see

Between Bouleaux Wood and the site of the Quadrilateral is the Dickens Cross, commemorating Major Cedric Dickens, the grandson of the famous author, killed nearby on 9 September and whose body was never recovered. The cross was replaced in 1995 and the original cross can be seen in the church at Ginchy. The impressive Guards Division Memorial is a kilometre from Ginchy on the Lesboeufs road and provides an excellent panorama of the September 1916 area. There is a memorial on the Flers road to the French *18ème R.I.T.* who fought in the surrounding area on 26 September 1914.

The Guards Cemetery at Lesboeufs has 3,136 graves. Nearby is a private memorial to Captain Meakin of the 3rd Coldstream Guards who was killed there on 25 September 1916.

John Philip Morton Carpenter, killed at Flers, 15 September 1916. He is buried in Bulls Road Cemetery.

An Australian officer in Gird Trench near Guedecourt, December 1916.

What to see

A.I.F. Burial Ground Cemetery has 3,475 Commonwealth burials. A Caribou stands on the ridge beyond Guedecourt and is the same as the one at Newfoundland Park. The Newfoundland Regiment captured a strongpoint here on 12 October 1916. The traces of original trenches can be seen. There are five Caribou monuments to this regiment on the Western Front.

At the junction with the D197 is a memorial to the French *82ème Division Territoriale* whose regiments fought at Morval, Ginchy and Flers on 26 September 1914. In the centre of Flers is the 41st Division Memorial. On the ridge between High Wood and Delville Wood is the New Zealand Division Memorial. Bulls Road Cemetery has 776 Commonwealth burials.

The village of Maurepas was the scene of terrible fighting in August-September 1916. The shrapnel-pierced water tower is a remarkable survivor of the 1916 fighting.

The hamlet of Frégicourt was totally destroyed during the fighting and never rebuilt. Its emplacement is today marked by an information panel on the D172 between Combles and Sailly-Saillisel.

SAILLY-SAILLISEL – RANCOURT

The fact that the 1916 battles of the Somme also involved a huge French contribution is often overlooked. Relationships between the allied forces were not always smooth and strategic cooperation not always present. However, the battles in the sectors where the two armies met relied on some form of cooperation and the British advance depended on French progress and vice-versa.

The French advance in the Combles region was along a south-north axis via the village of Maurepas and along the L'hôpital – Le Forest ravine. The small wood of Anderlu was taken by the *8ème R.I.* on 12 September. The German strongpoint of Le Priez farm was captured the following day by the *33ème R.I.*, creating a pronounced salient in the line and now occupying high ground that overlooked the valley in which Combles lay. On 25 September and in conjunction with the British advance on their left flank, the French *1ère D.I.* attacked towards Frégicourt with the *42ème D.I.* advancing towards Rancourt. Following the fall of Combles, the French continued their attack beyond Rancourt and on towards Sailly-Saillisel and the huge wood of Saint-Pierre Vaast. The battle raged on here throughout October and November. Sailly-Saillisel fell to the *15ème R.I.* on 12 November but a German counter-attack two days later pushed the French back again, including the western corner of the Saint-Pierre-Waast wood.

A small aluminium bottle marked 'souvenir du bois danderlu' (sic) and the small shell splinter that pierced it. This wood was attacked by the 8ème R.I. on 12 September 1916. The regiment hailed from the St.Omer region and they suffered heavy losses in taking the wood. The wood is on the high ground above Combles alongside the motorway and still bears the traces of the fighting.

What to see

There is much to see in this part of the battlefields. On the D146 road is a private memorial to Victor Hallard of the *110ème R.I.* Continuing on this road will take you Maurepas, the ground to the left before the village is the ravine of L'Hôpital and Le Forest where the French lost so many men in taking two German trenches that ran along the high ground on the other side. Maurepas has a large French military cemetery containing the remains of 3,657 soldiers of the *1ère R.I.* Leaving Combles on the D20 is another memorial to Charles Dansette of the *43ème R.I.*
The Combles-Sailly-Saillisel road takes you past the site of the former hamlet of Frégicourt. There is a memorial opposite to *l'abbé* J. Boisson who was killed there in October 1916.
Rancourt has a large French memorial chapel housing hundreds of privately-funded plaques to men who lost their lives on the Somme in 1914-1918. A large cemetery containing 5,327 graves and a further 3,223 French soldiers in four ossuaries is adjacent to the chapel. There is also a large German cemetery containing the remains of 11,422 soldiers.

The main square in Péronne in March 1917.

British officers of the 48th (South Midland) Division in Péronne. The Division entered the town on 18 March 1917.

PÉRONNE

The town of Péronne was first captured and occupied by the Germans in late August 1914. Following their defeat on the Marne, the Germans pulled back from the Somme and Péronne was once more in French hands. However, the relief felt by the population was short-lived and the Germans returned late September with the town remaining in their hands until they withdrew to the Hindenburg Line in March 1917. Whereas Bapaume, a town further north, became the focus of the British advance, Péronne became the objective of the French push along the river Somme. The nearby villages of Cléry and Bouchavesnes saw terrible losses on both sides. South of the river and on the outskirts of Péronne, the French were halted at Biaches.

British troops of the 48th (South Midland) Division entered Péronne on 18 March 1917. The Germans had put into action *Operation Alberich*, a planned withdrawal to a new defensive line, the *Siegfriedstellung* (Hindenburg Line). This operation was planned when Falkenhayn was replaced as chief of general staff in September 1916 by Hindenburg and Ludendorff. It would shorten the front by 40 kilometres and free up 14 infantry divisions which were sorely needed as German losses on the Somme reached were approximately 500,000 men. *Alberich* was carried out from 9 February to 20 March.

The Germans adopted a scorched earth policy as they withdrew, cutting down trees, destroying buildings and poisoning wells.

The Germans were back in Péronne on 23 March 1918 and remained there until the 1 September when Australian troops entered the town. Mont St. Quentin, just north of Péronne was an important German strongpoint captured by the 2nd Australian Division against units of the German *51. Korps* between 31 August and 3 September 1918.

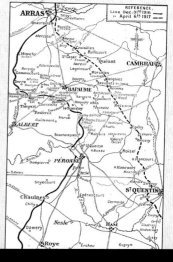

The German withdrawal to the Hindenburg Line. The German withdrawal to the Hindenburg Line.

What to see

The town is home to the excellent Historial de Péronne museum of the Great War which looks at all aspects of the conflict, including social as well as military aspects. The 2nd Australian Memorial is on nearby Mont St. Quentin on the Péronne-Bapaume road, nearby is also a new Remembrance trail with remains of trenches, recently set up by the Historial of Péronne. By continuing on this road you will come to Bouchavesnes Bergen, a small village which saw some of the costliest fighting for the French on the Somme in 1916. There is a monument to Foch who was the French commander on the Somme in 1916. In nearby Moislans is a small French cemetery for men of the Charentes region who fell in the fighting here on 28 August 1914. They were part of the *307ème régiment d'infanterie*, a unit formed with reservists who only twenty-four days earlier had been going about their civilian occupations.

A French gas attack in progress at L'Echelle St. Aurin in the southern Somme sector. 12 July 1916.

BIACHES – BARLEUX – BELLOY-EN-SANTERRE

The American poet Alan Seeger who voluntarily enlisted with the French Foreign Legion. He was killed at Belloy-en-Santerre on 4 July 1916.

The French attack on 1 July south of the Somme was launched two hours later than the Franco-British offensive north of the river. After a week-long artillery bombardment, the 1ère Corps Colonial and the 35ème Corps d'Armée began their offensive across the Santerre plateau between the river Somme and Flaucourt in the south. By starting the attack at 9.30 a.m., the French achieved a certain element of surprise. The next day the village of Frise on the river had fallen, as well as the woods dominating the southern side of the valley. Buscourt, Flaucourt and Assevillers were captured on the 3 July. Belloy-en-Santerre and Estrees fell the following day, then Hem and the fortified Monacu farm. By 10 July the French 6ème Armée had advanced along a twenty kilometre front to a depth that reached in some sectors ten kilometres. It had captured over 12,000 prisoners and a huge quantity of artillery pieces and machine-guns. Unlike the bulk of the British forces further north, the French had greater offensive experience and used fire and movement techniques using small units that would later be emulated by their allied counterparts.

Biaches

The village of Biaches, on the other side of the river Somme on the outskirts of Péronne was reached by the French 164ème R.I. on 9 July. The line did not move any further and the village and the high ground of La Maisonnette overlooking Péronne were the scene of extremely heavy fighting. La Maisonnette was lost and recaptured seven times and it is estimated that more shells per square metre fell there than on the Verdun battlefield.

What to see

The French military cemetery at Biaches contains the graves of 1,040 men and the remains of a further 322 rench soldiers in two ossuaries.

A rail-mounted French long range artillery gun on the Somme in 1916.

"The whole position was just one great field of corpses. The weather was hot, there was little water to be had and over everything there hung the appalling, sickly-sweet stench of decomposition." Regimental historian, German Fusilier Regiment 40, La Maisonnette (Biaches), August 1916.

Barleux

The small village of Barleux is approximately five kilometres south-west of Biaches. It was reached by French colonial troops on 9 July but was strongly defended by *I.R. 89.* which held onto its positions until being forced back on 20 July. The village itself, however, still remained in German hands. German *Grenadier-Regiment 89* held off sustained French attacks throughout August and fended off a heavy attack on 4 September. Barleux was finally occupied by the French on 17 March 1917 following the German withdrawal to the Hindenburg Line.

Belloy-en-Santerre

This village lies a few kilometres to the south-west of Barleux. It was captured, along with other nearby villages, on 25 September 1914 by Bavarian troops of the *2. Infanterie-Division*. The village was attacked and captured by the *4ème Régiment de Marche de la Légion Etrangère* on 4 July 1916.

One of the Legionnaires was the American poet and former Harvard student, Alan Seeger. He is known for his poem, I have a rendezvous with death. His body was never found.

What to see

There is a plaque on the village war memorial to the *4ème R.M.L.E.* which lost 700 men killed in the battle for Belloy-en-Santerre. The town square is named after Alan Seeger and there is a small commemorative plaque on the town hall.

THE GERMAN SPRING OFFENSIVES 1918

Following the German withdrawal to the Hindenburg Line in February-March 1917, the Allies kept up the pressure with a British offensive at Arras on 9 April, followed by the French along the Chemin des Dames a week later. The French attack was a disaster and the terrible casualties led to a series of refusals by certain regiments to be sacrificed in such a wanton fashion. The French armies were in dire need of rest and overhaul ; they had, up to the Somme offensive, borne the bulk of the fighting, especially in 1915 and Verdun in 1916.

It now fell upon the British to bear the bulk of the fighting. Fresh offensives were undertaken at Messines in June, then at Ypres between the end of July and mid-November, followed by a final attack at Cambrai. The German high command decided that a knock-out blow needed to be dealt before the Americans arrived and tip the balance in favour of the Allies. With the Russians now out of the war, the Germans could send their Eastern Front divisions to the west. The Germans decided to attack the British Expeditionary Force as they considered it to be exhausted from its offensives of 1917.

The state of the British Expeditionary Force in March 1918

The battles of 1917 had left the BEF in a state of exhaustion, Passchendaele especially had dented morale, as well as the German counter-attack at Cambrai at the end of November. Politics also played a role. British Prime Minister, Lloyd-George accepted to take over more frontline from the French across an area that was not ready for defence in depth. The War Office also told the British Commander-in-Chief, Sir Douglas Haig, that he could not expect replacement troops to make up the shortfall in manpower. British divisions were also sent to Italy to assist their ally following the devastating defeat at Caporetto in October-November. The British would also now have to learn to fight a defensive battle. The manpower crisis led the BEF to reduce the size of its infantry brigades from four to three battalions. All of this happened at a time when it was obvious that the

Germans were growing in strength in order to launch a final attack.

The German army

The German attack was planned to fall along a 70 kilometre front between Arras in the north, St.Quentin and La Fère, but the main weight of the attack would be between Arras and St. Quentin. The Germans had at their disposal 74 infantry divisions and over 6,000 artillery pieces.

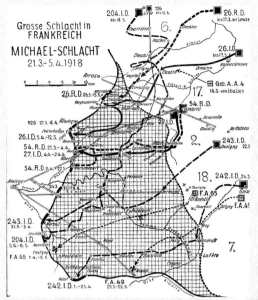

The German Michael offensive.

THE ATTACK, 21 MARCH 1918

The German bombardment started at 4.35 a.m. along a 60 kilometre front, with vital supply routes far beyond the frontline subjected to long-range artillery fire. Five minutes later, a heavy barrage hit British lines south-west of St. Quentin. In the space of five hours, three and a half million shells were fired. Winston Churchill, Minister of Munitions at the time, was visiting a division at Nurlu when the barrage began : *"..there rose in less than one minute the most tremendous cannonade I shall ever hear...It swept round us in a wide curve of red leaping flame stretching to the north far along the front of the 3rd Army, as well as the 5th Army in the south, and quite unending in either direction."*

formed elite stormtroop units for such a task, taking the best elements of various units in order to create these shock divisions.

By the end of the day, the Germans had penetrated south-west of St. Quentin and also against the 3rd Army sector on the Cambrai-Bapaume road, the 59th Division had been pushed back in the Bullecourt sector.

The deep barrage had effectively knocked out the British ability to respond to the attack. The German infantry began localised attacks at 5.30 a.m. but the main started at 9 a.m. using tactics already used on the Eastern Front. This consisted of infiltration, pushing through gaps in the British defences and advancing, leaving any areas of resistance to be mopped up by units following the main assault. The Germans had

The town of Albert fell during the night of 26/27 March. The German troops were amazed at the quantity of stores, food and equipment they captured as their own propaganda had told them that the Allies were in the same depleted state as they were. The realisation that this was not true did much to damage German morale.

A captured British redoubt, 21 March 1918.

March 22-25

The British continued to withdraw although some redoubts still held out, sometimes to the last man. By the 23rd, the Germans were at the canal at Jussy and further north, were at Bapaume and the former 1916 battlefields. Haig met with the French commander-in-chief Pétain who believed that the British 5th Army was defeated. Under pressure from his own government, he wanted to pull his armies back to Beauvais and protect Paris. Faced with this worrying development, Haig called for an allied conference.

March 26

The conference was held in the town hall at Doullens* in the presence of the French president and prime minister as well as senior allied generals. It was decided to make Foch the commander of allied forces on the Western Front. French troops would now be sent in to bolster the British 5th Army.

March 27

This day saw fighting at Rosières on the southern part of the Somme battlefield; the Germans were now only 30 kilometres from Amiens and had swept across the 1916 areas that had taken so much allied sacrifice to win. The town of Albert fell, as did the vital French-held road hub of Montdidier further south. The line, however, began to hold as reinforcements arrived, notably the New Zealand Division near Beaumont-Hamel and the Australians towards the Albert area.

German Stormtrooper equipment.

Australian and American troops at Le Hamel after the victorious attack of 4 July.

VILLERS-BRETONNEUX

Just after the Doullens Conference, Haig was shocked to learn that VII Corps, following a misinterpretation in orders, had pulled back from Bray to take up positions along the Ancre, thus creating a gap and opening the way for the Germans to push on to Amiens. The Australian Corps, held in reserve, was brought into the line and stopped the Germans at Dernancourt near Albert, as well as ground near Corbie and a town that would be forever linked with Australia, Villers-Bretonneux.

The Germans attacked again on 4 April, capturing Le Hamel. The Australian 1st Division remained in the north where a new German offensive was launched on 9 April. The other four divisions held the line between Dernancourt to Villers-Bretonneux. Eventually, British reinforcements arrived, whose extreme youth came as a shock to the Australians. The Germans launched a huge attack against Villers-Bretonneux on 24 April, supported by tanks and flame-throwers. The town was captured and the first ever tank-on-tank engagement took place. At 10 p.m., a counter-attack was launched by two Australian and one British infantry brigade. After hand-to-hand fighting, the town was cleared. The vital rail-hub of Amiens had been saved.

Fighting continued in the vicinity of the town for several months. The German offensive in this sector came to an end at the end of April as they prepared fresh attacks on French-held parts of the Western Front.

1918 artillery fire damage is still visible in Corbie.

Le Hamel

The German-held area on the high ground around Le Hamel formed a bulge in the frontline and allowed good observation across the allied lines. An attack was launched on 4 July 1918 by the 4th Australian Division, as well as brigades from the 2nd and 3rd Australian Divisions, and several infantry companies from the US 131st and 132nd Infantry Regiments, 33rd Division. The attack was a success and achieved its objectives within ninety minutes. Le Hamel was a triumph of planning on the part of John Monash, the Australian Corps commander since May. He put into action all that had been previously learnt in hard-fought battles and his combined arms tactics involving artillery, infantry, tanks and aircraft would play a vital role in the final battles of the war.

German A7V tank 'Mephisto' was in action at Villers-Bretonneux on 24 April. It was recovered by the Australians and eventually shipped back home and displayed at the Queensland Museum.

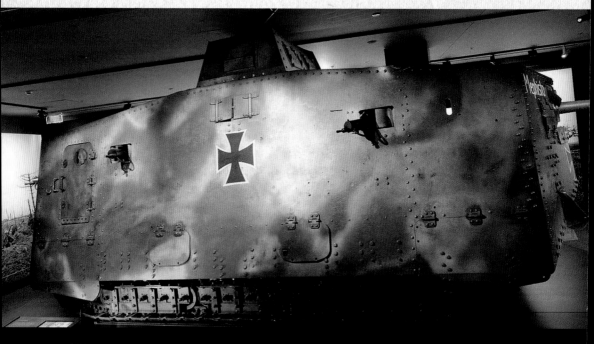

What to see

Villers-Bretonneux is home to the Australian National Monument on Hill 104 on the road to Corbie. It was inaugurated in 1938 and bears the names of 10,770 Australians who died on the Western Front and who have no known grave. A new John Monash visitors centre is due to open here in 2018. The town itself has a Franco-Australian Museum in the school building which was funded by school children from the state of Victoria after the war. A kilometre along the D168 to Cachy is a small monument commemorating the first ever tank-versus-tank battle of 24 April 1918.

At Le Hamel is the Australian Corps Memorial Park and information panels explaining this important battle as well as the role played by the Corps on the Western Front. The nearby town of Corbie was home to casualty clearing stations during the 1916 battles. Shell fire damage can still be seen on the St. Pierre abbey. Leaving on the D1 road will bring you to a brickworks and chimney after 3 kms. An information panel shows that this was the crash site of Baron Manfred von Richtofen on 21 April 1918. Another 3 kms brings you to the 3rd Australian Division Memorial and fabulous views across the Somme valley.

THE BATTLE OF AMIENS AND THE HUNDRED DAYS OFFENSIVE

The Germans launched more offensives against the French along the Chemin des Dames and the Marne but despite initial success, they only served to wear down their own infantry divisions. The French were the first to hit back on the Marne on 18 July, pushing the Germans back across the ground they had gained in May-June.

The next allied offensive came on 8 August with the line running from the Ancre River in the north to the Avre River north of Montdidier. British, Canadian, Australian and French divisions pushed the Germans back as far as 13 kms on the first day. The attack continued until 13 August, but despite demands by the French to continue, Haig refused, preferring instead to prepare a second offensive between the Ancre and Scarpe rivers.

21 August saw the start of the next offensive, Albert was recaptured the next day, Bapaume a week later, and the Australians were in Péronne on 1 September. The old 1916 battlefields had been crossed for the last time. The Germans fell back to their former Hindenburg Line positions. The department of the Somme would see no further fighting but there would be more hard-fought actions before the Armistice of 11 November.

A British infantryman of the 17th (Northern) Division, August 1918. A volunteer in September 1914 who answered Lord Kitchener's call to arms, this man arrived in France in July 1915. His first taste of action was near Ypres in March 1916, then in the summer of 1916 at Fricourt, Contalmaison, Longueval and Guedecourt. 1917 saw him at Arras, then the 3rd Battle of Ypres at Langemarck. Pushed back by the German 21 March offensive, he fought rear-guard actions across the Somme before reaching Albert. His battalion, the 6th Dorsetshires, pushed the Germans out of Thiepval on 24 August and then across the old 1916 battlefields.

17th (Northern) Division insignia. The dot and dash represent the top of the one and seven.

RECONSTRUCTION

The nineteen-twenties and thirties were also a time for remembering the dead. The Franco-British Memorial of Thiepval is seen here during its construction in 1931. It was inaugurated in the summer of 1932.

Four years of war had left the department of the Somme with some areas having been wiped off the map. Parts of the 1916 and 1918 battlefields were classified as *Zone Rouge*, that is to say, too destroyed and dangerous to be rebuilt or restored for agricultural use. Towns such as Albert had been important pre-war centres of manufacture and factories would need to be rebuilt in order to restart economic activity. Before the war the Somme had almost seventy thousand farms and the Santerre plateau had produced large quantities of wheat and sugar beet. The French authorities had looked into the problem of post war agriculture as early as 1917, Henri Hutier wrote that..."*Where there had been villages one sees nothing but shellholes and trenches, not a square metre of top soil is in place, everything has been disturbed....*".

However, the tough people of Picardy returned and set to turning the prairie-like wasteland back to farming, ignoring the fact that many areas had been designated *Zone Rouge*. Reparation money was yet to be received and in some areas the returning populations even lived in old dugouts before temporary housing was made available. Help was also made available by various British and American charitable organisations.

The British military presence remained for many years after the Armistice. Battlefield clearance units worked with Chinese Labour Corps men and German prisoners in clearing away unexploded ammunition. The old trench lines and crater fields were combed over in search of the missing.

Many Somme villages and towns were adopted by British towns and cities, Albert was also adopted by Bordeaux and the Chinese town of Tianjin.

Post war temporary housing can still be seen in some villages, such as here in Guillemont.

Somme timeline

The Somme saw fighting throughout the four years of the war. The first battles occurred as early as late August 1914, barely more than three weeks after the outbreak of the war.

Late August 1914, the first fighting takes place on the Somme. Péronne, Albert and Amiens fall.

Late September, after the fighting on the Marne, both sides seek to outflank each other. Heavy fighting along the entire Somme area. The frontline settles and trench lines are dug.

19 December 1914, French attacks are repulsed in many areas of the Somme, losses are heavy.

June 1915, further French attacks take place to support attacks in the Artois region.

July-August 1915. The first British divisions take over from the French in the Somme. The junction with the French army is at the village of Maricourt.

December 1915. An inter-allied conference decides on a Franco-British offensive in the Somme for the following summer.

21 February 1916, the Germans attack at Verdun.

24 June 1916. The artillery preparation for the Franco-British offensive begins.

1 July 1916. The first day of the Somme. Huge British losses for little gain. The French make great gains south of the river Somme and along the Santerre plateau.

14 July 1916. A successful British attack takes Bazentin Ridge. Heavy fighting takes place throughout the summer. The Australians take Pozières. Terrible fighting at High and Delville Wood.

15 September. A huge offensive succeeds in capturing the villages of Courcelette, Martinpuich and Flers. Tanks are used for the first time. The French push on towards Combles but are halted south of the river Somme at Biaches and along the Santerre plateau.

26 September. The German fortress of Thiepval falls to the British 18th Division.

13 November. Beaumont Hamel is captured. The British push along the Ancre valley towards Grandcourt. The French are involved in heavy fighting at Sailly Saillisel and the wood of St. Pierre Vaast. The onset of winter brings the offensive to a close.

February-March 1917. The Germans begin a tactical withdrawal towards the Hindenburg Line in the east.

21 March 1918. The German Michael offensive pushes the British 5th Army back across the former Somme battlefields.

April 1918. Australian and British forces halt the German advance on Amiens at Villers-Bretonneux. The Australians recapture the small town towards the end of the month.

8 August 1918. The Battle of Amiens. French, Canadian, Australian and British forces launch a successful offensive, capturing tens of thousands of German troops.

August – September, the Hundred Days offensive finally pushes the Germans out of the Somme.

SOMME COMMUNITIES ADOPTED BY BRITISH TOWNS AND CITIES

Birmingham	Albert	Leyton	Authuille
Brighouse	Courcelette	Maidstone	Montauban-de-Picardie
Burnley	Miraumont, Colincamps	Melbourne (Australia)	Villers-Bretonneux
Canterbury	Lesbœufs	Portsmouth	Combles, Flers
Derby	Foncquevillers, Barleux	Sandwich	Framerville-Rainecourt
Exeter	Montdidier	Southampton	Gueudecourt, Martinpuich
Folkestone	Morlancourt	Stourbridge	Grandcourt
Gloucester	Ovillers, La Boisselle	Tonbridge	Thiepval
Hornsey	Guillemont	Warwick	Longavesnes
Ipswich	Bazentin, Fricourt	Winchester	Mailly-Maillet, Auchonvillers,
Jersey	Soyécourt		Beaumont-Hamel

ELEVÉ EN 1925
AVEC LE CONCOURS DE
NOTRE MARRAINE ANGLAISE
LA VILLE DE MAIDSTONE

A plaque on the water tower at Montauban.

Commonwealth War Graves Commission cemetery signs near the village of Serre.

ACKNOWLEDGEMENTS

The history of the Great War is one of my great passions and has led to many wonderful encounters and friendships. I would like to say a big thank you to my wonderful wife Sally and our children who have to put up with a husband and father who often seems to live in the period of 1914-1918.

I would also like to convey my gratitude to fellow collectors and friends who have helped me with photos for this publication : Kate and Martin Pegler, Faris Siwadi, Sven Kuczyk, René Senteur, Marc le Moal, Merlijn van Eijk, Antoine Berthe, Christophe Damiens, Sophie Carluer and the Le Maitre family, Claudie Llewellyn and Peter Scott. Special thanks also go to Peter Bull for allowing me to use some of his beautiful photos of the battlefields today.

Lastly, I would like to dedicate this modest publication to all those whose lives fell under the shadow of the Great War, be it on the front line, behind the lines, in factories or those who lived in fear of the knock at the door. A special dedication is made to the wonderful people of Picardy who do so much today in order to perpetuate the memory of the men who fought in their villages and fields.